MW00559536

# ENGINEERING FOR KIDS
## Building and Construction Fun
## Children's Engineering Books

SPEEDY
PUBLISHING

Speedy Publishing LLC
40 E. Main St. #1156
Newark, DE 19711
www.speedypublishing.com

Copyright 2015

All Rights reserved. No part of this book may be reproduced or used in any way or form or by any means whether electronic or mechanical, this means that you cannot record or photocopy any material ideas or tips that are provided in this book

**Engineering is the use of science and math to design or make things.**

People who do engineering are called engineers.

The word engineer comes from a Latin word meaning 'cleverness'.

**Engineers usually design or build things that are sold or given to people.**

**Construction is the process of creating and building infrastructure or a facility.**

Construction starts with planning, design, financing and continues until the project is built and ready for use.

The first buildings were huts and shelters, constructed by hand or with simple tools.

**Modern construction is consistently made of materials such as glass, steel, concrete and bricks.**

All building construction projects include some elements in common - design, financial, estimating and legal considerations.

A formal design team may be assembled to plan the physical proceedings.

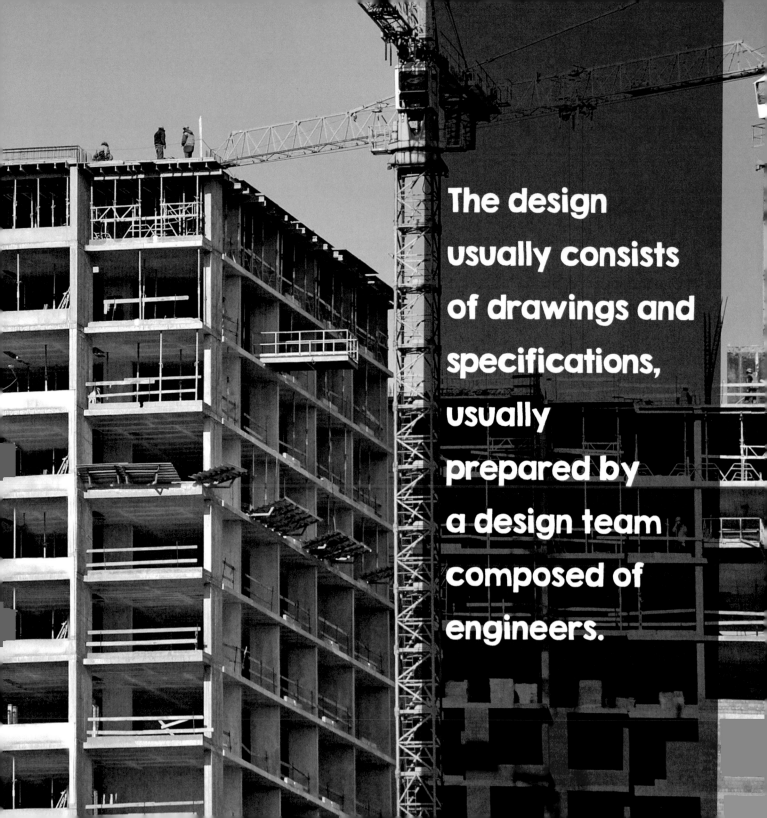

The design usually consists of drawings and specifications, usually prepared by a design team composed of engineers.

Once the design is completed, a number of construction companies may then be asked to make a bid for the work.

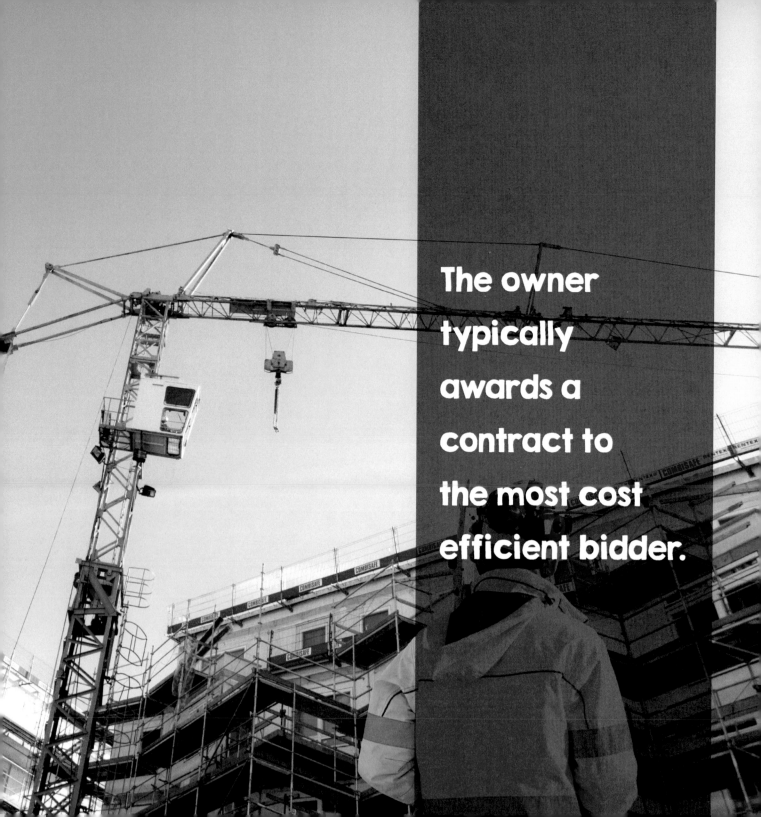

The owner typically awards a contract to the most cost efficient bidder.

A construction worker is someone whose job is to work on a construction site.

Construction workers use many types of tools and operate machines and vehicles.

Construction
workers
have to wear
safety clothing
to protect
themselves.

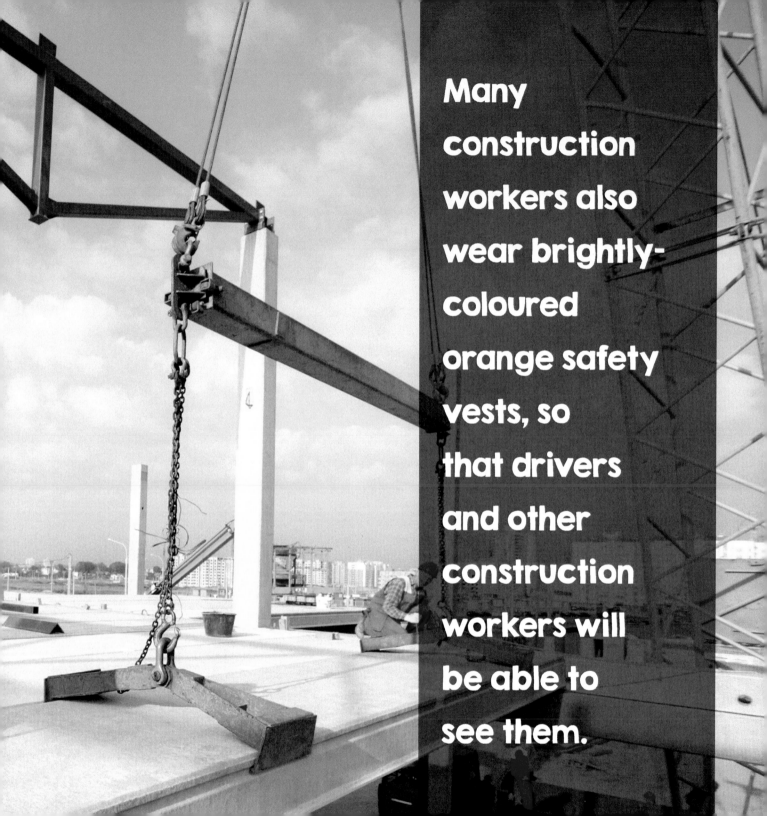

Many construction workers also wear brightly-coloured orange safety vests, so that drivers and other construction workers will be able to see them.

Construction
is one of the
most dangerous
occupations
in the world.

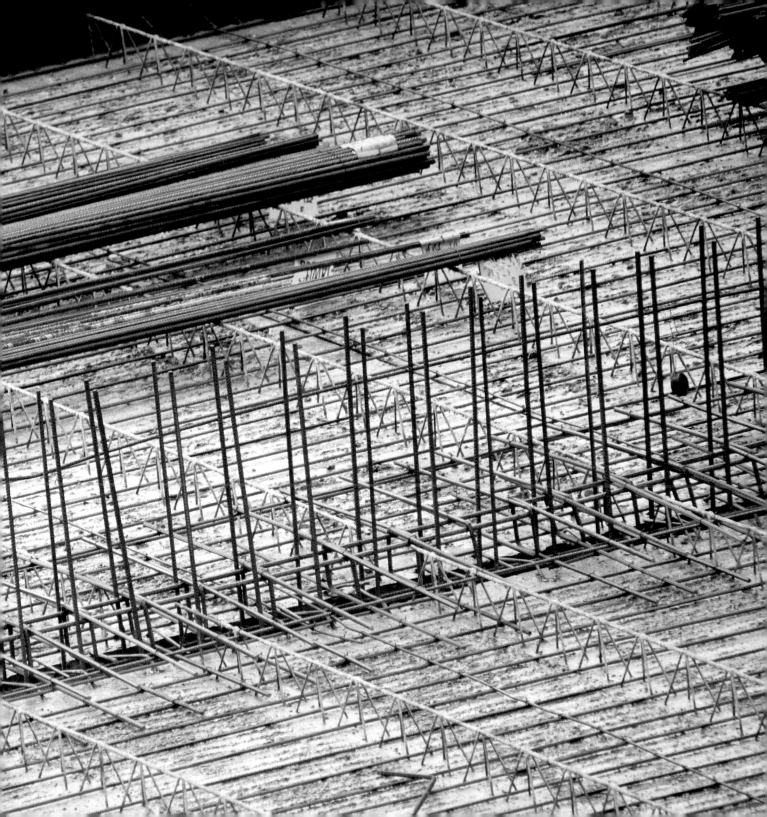

Made in the USA
Middletown, DE
31 March 2019

40780235R00024